Beneath the Surface

A Poet's Reflection

Teri Dourmashkin Ed.D

While every precaution has been taken in the preparation of this book, the publisher assumes no responsibility for errors or omissions, or for damages resulting from the use of the information contained herein.

BENEATH THE SURFACE

First edition. April 20, 2024.

ISBN: 979-8224275632

Written by Teri Dourmashkin.

I dedicate this book to every person who is brave enough to face their inner demons, their darkness, without judgment and with bravery and courage.Self-growth and healing require that we delve deep into our hearts and souls; to accept ourselves as we are yet having the willingness to walk the path of self-love, so we learn to embrace our imperfections, our vulnerabilities, and our past hearts and traumas.It is the realization that if we choose, we will always be a work in progress. In the end it is about love.First love of self, and then taking that love and extending it to others.

I tenderly hold your heart in my hands.
Please take mine and hold it in yours.
Feeling so safe, a sweet ocean's roar.
Come read me poetry, we'll sit in the sand.

Don't give up on love, it's never too late.
Romance is blooming, holding hands by a lake.
Don't worry if you are fifty or eighty-two.
You deserve sweet kisses, passions gate.
Open your heart, let yourself be wooed.
Unleash your desires, trust your sweet fate.

Floating in sunshine, waters deep azure blue.
Your care for me, so splendid and true.
feel your touch, my spirit renewed.
You pierce my heart; my soul is on fire.
You awaken my deepest, buried desires.
Come run away with me, never look back.
Falling into your arms, there is nothing I lack.

I love you with all my heart and soul.
Was hurt so much, gutted, and torn.
Trust in tatters, bitter winters so cold.
You understood, faith slowly reborn.
I want you with every breath I behold.
I blossom, I awake, silky new morn.

I feel your love deeply, azure blue oceans floor.
Symphonies of tenderness, passion and more.
Love songs you whisper, my heart wants to soar.
Dive into my soul, many folds to explore.
Come let me kiss you, it's you I adore.

\.*~♡~*./

My heart is racing, I think of your words.
Etched onto my body, flooded with love.
Symphonic melodies such passions it stirs.
I vibrate all over, such soft silky gloves.
Come to me now, fly away hummingbirds.
Kiss me forever, moonlight, stars above.

\.*~ ♡ ~*./

I have no more words, just frozen on ice.
I expose my angst, my suffering, my plight.
My words are not for the timid, I may pay a price.
My sadness lies deep, been too many years.
Haunted and covered, deep mist, hovering tears.
I must have my freedom, not a roll of the dice.

\.*~ ♡ ~*./

Make yourself vulnerable, why not just share?
If you stand in judgment, it is not yours to bear.
Takes courage to expose, not light air.
Just be yourself, no shame, no despair.

I think of your softness,
I think of your touch.
Wake me up in the morning, your kiss means so much.
Make love to my soul, my heart, my mind.
I can hold you forever, throughout all time.
Your words make me shiver, sweet passion erupts.

\.*~ ♡ ~*./

Dig deep inside the depths of your soul.
Are you a young one, or incredibly old?
Breathe in the softness, divinity's touch.
A kindred spirit, an eternal blush.
Feeling the moon dipped in the sun.
All God's creations: we are all one.

You run your fingers through my hair,
You read me poetry, such love, such care.
You ignite my passions; a rebirth has sprung.
I want to kiss you till the earth hits the sun.
Your love for me such rarefied air.
I've waited a lifetime, we've only begun.

My faith is shaken, feeling beat up.
Climbing up mountains, I cannot even touch.
Frustration beating on suns with no flames.
Stretched to my limits, pain's wicked game.
Digging in tunnels, hidden treasures I clutch.
God give me the strength; I must not give up.

You see right through my heart and soul.
I want to hold hands when we are old.
Soft crashing waves your lips touch mine.
I have waited so long, moments so divine.
Obstacles are just lessons, to have and to hold.
Have faith my love, just a matter of time.

You whisper to me sweet songs of love,
I look at the heavens and thank God above.
Your heart and mine, a starlit glove.
You move me in ways, speechless in love.
You pierce my soul down to my core.
Enraptured on fire, it is you I adore.

Do you fear the darkness inside your soul?
Do you fear becoming old?
Do you fear spinning tapes inside your head?
Do you fear dark clouds sobbing with dread?
Fear is a firestorm that burns your heart.
Let it go, let it go, make a fresh start.

Come to me in my dream's softest night.
You are the one to make all things right.
Fingers lost in my hair; I swoon with delight.
So sexy, so romantic, loves magical flight.
I have waited for you many lifetimes ago.
Come, let us dip in sweet silky snow.

When I was young, steel armors I wore.
Did not get to close, shame buried ashore.
Fear of abandonment ripped, and it tore.
Not mine to begin with, rigid steel floors.
I've come a long way down to my core.
My heart is now open, swinging open the door.

\.*~ ♡ ~*./

Floating alone in an endless sea.
I close my eyes and see victory.
The clouds overcast, feeling strong and free.
I am my own savior, celestial symphonies.

\.*~ ♡ ~*./

You are your own savior.
Dive deep into the sea.
So many tunnels, such mystery.
Your God given gift; self-discovery.
Healing is a long journey, let yourself be.

I need to feel loved, safe, and secure.
I need to breathe air along ocean shores.
I need to feel peaceful and not just endure.
I need your love, please open new doors.
I need your solace like never before.
I need my freedom, like a butterfly I soar.

Can't take it anymore.
Heart drained to my core.
Symptoms running wild,
Exhausted, no more smiles.
No empathy I crave, just peaceful shores.
Brain keeps on fighting, slamming steel doors.
No words left to say, tomorrow's a new day.

She's an open book.
She let go of the shame,
Reflections in a mirror, please take a look.
We are the same, not an overwhelming game.
Our humanity is real, please honor your name.

\\.*~ ♡ ~*./

My spirits are lifted by such beautiful souls.
Your kindness, a gift I am blessed to behold.
My heart is so humbled, your beauty unfolds.
Your love brings such comfort, previous pure gold.

You grace me with such kindness and care.
Your love unconditional, a breath of fresh air.
So much abuse, disrespect, shattered tears.
Still sitting in dust, beyond my repair.
Patience wraps me in Divine prayer.
Holding hands softly throughout all the years.

Trapped within these four walls.
Tearless tears flood tile floors.
Pain is a demon, a thief with a knife.
So much emotion, banging on doors.
A presence in my life, I cannot escape.
I must find my peace, not up for debate.

If you could dive into the depths of love.
Your understanding would fly like a dove.
All dark lingering's would be erased.
Standing at the doorway to heaven's gate.

I do all I can to get through the pain.
Torrents and torrents of pouring rain.
How do these words even make the page?
Secrets tunnel ways in my brain, in a daze.
I lift through the fog; poetry bears my name.
My words, pen and paper are not in vain.

Sometimes left speechless, whispering love words.
They dance into my heart, a sweet hummingbird.
They take me to places, I swoon, and I melt.
You dive into my soul songs yet to be heard.
Your kindness a flame, longings I've never felt.
I want you right now, such passion you've stirred.

He gazes at me in the fine sun.
A love so gentle, flowers have sprung.
I dance on moonlight, stardust in my hair.
I dream upon oceans, so calming night air.
Feel my soul like you never have dared.

Depression cuts through my very core.
Some days I feel it, slam all the doors.
Pain screams lightning and thunder bolts.
I write these words, let the bleeding pour.
Verses so dreary too much of a jolt.
I am just human, one day I will float.

Every door is being slammed in my face.
My hope running out, alone and displaced.
Pseudo God's in white coats, not even a trace.
Locked in this desert, such barren waste.
Where is my haven, my solace, my grace?
Tomorrow's a new day, another time and place.

I long for the day when my hand touches yours.
Our souls are connected, deep down to our cores.
Obstacles and challenges, mountains that roar.
We have to have faith; our love will endure.
Life's full of magic, kissing waves at the shore.

Every once in a while, your heart skips a beat.
Could come from anywhere, emotions run deep.
Can be from love, knocking on your door.
The one who will love you forever more.
It can be for self-love that fills up your soul.
It is never too late; you are never too old.

\.*~ ♡ ~*./

I dream of being light as air.
Throw away the struggles, the obstacles, the fear.
Crying inside, wipe away all the tears.
Floating on clouds at early dawn's break.
Am I sleeping or really awake?
Come and touch me, you make my heart quake.

Withering into a soul gone lost.
My stomach is churning, melt all the frost.
My solace, my dreams I count on one hand.
I close my eyes float away, exotic land.
Will they happen or will they not?
My fate in God's hands, tick tock, tick tock.

If you can't be authentic, then what do you got?
A soul that is stifled, stuck in box.
Crawling and crying untie the knot.
Your expression is magic, did you forget?
Let that ink dry on the page,
Your words have power, today's a new day.

Do you think you know me?
Do you know my heart?
We are all connected, right from the start.
To live is to be human, arms open wide.
Give love to one another, stop this divide.

Tear down your mask,
Let down those walls,
You won't be in danger,
Cleansing waterfalls.
Let us see you...nothing to hide.
Wash away all the shame,
Self-love is your pride.

I yearn for a love so sacred and rare.
I hold out my hands, are you really there?
So many years clutching heartache and pain.
Come into my arms, cleanse my heart, pouring rain.
Melt into my soul, wipe away all the stains.
I have waited a lifetime, please whisper my name.

I want to breathe in sweet loving air.
My struggles are many, my body in tears.
I want my life back, many tormented years.
Locked in chains, they rebel, they don't care.
I want simple things, swept away by a storm.
I pray for my life, please God have it restored.

I want you; I need you, every breath I take.
Lift me out from this slumber, darkest of days.
You pull at my heart strings; from despair I awake.
A kindness of spirit never known before.
I close my eyes, see magical doors.
Take my hand, we'll forever explore.

Give love to strangers, a smile may heal their day.
This world not the same, distractions texting away.
Human connection, a feel a sweet touch,
Has gone by the wayside, have you had enough?
Look into somebody's eyes, feel their heartache.
Make human connection, let us awake.

Many sides to me, contradictions take hold.
A heart soft as silk, a voice mountain bold.
I am who I am, I embrace all of me.
I am my own savior, rough tides, calming seas.
Imperfectly beautiful, sometimes afraid midnight air.
Other times fearless, nary a care.

The midnight air so calming, no strain.
I close my eyes and dance in the rain.
I gaze at the stars; they call out my name.
They speak their own language filled with such grace.
Please transport me, another time and place.
My faith is my lifeboat, may I feel God's embrace.

My head is pained by many things.
A union that breathed its last breath.
My heart being jabbed darts and pins.
My body aches deepest of depths.
I write of darkness, let the light roll in.
Grant me my sanity, that is not a sin.

\.*~ ♡ ~*./

No matter how dark my words splatter with ink,
There is always a new day, faith always wins.
Rest your weary heads, you will not sink.
Life can be difficult, sharp sticking pins.
Never give up sipping heavenly drinks.

In a surprisingly good mood.
My head clear of pain.
I am blessed on these days,
I could dance in the rain.
Be grateful for everything,
Tiny moments give grace,
Live in the moment, a loving embrace.

\.*~ ♡ ~*./

Watercolors dipped in pastels kiss my face.
I close my eyes, transported another place.
I see Monet, a splash of beauty and grace.
I walk in Paris clinking cobbled stone streets.
A smile from strangers, what a heavenly greet.
Another century, or a dream, celestial gates.

Underappreciated, I fall from grace.
What is my purpose, my soul lost in space.
I'm screaming, I'm yelling, a ghost not a trace.
Lost on deaf ears, invisible tears.
Feeling unheard for so many years.
I awake from a nightmare, feeling displaced.

The flesh is only skin deep.
What's in one's heart is beauty to keep.
A body is beautiful, no matter what shape.
Yet the soul goes beyond adornments and capes.
Love goes inward, beyond a pretty face.

\.*~ ♡ ~*./

I am numb, I am sad.
I am afraid, sans all the tears.
Being mistreated, Deja vu, beyond mad.
Sometimes hopeless, been so many years.
I will win, I will seal my fate.
I will shut the door, will not hesitate.

\.*~ ♡ ~*./

Spill your guts.
Why should you care?
Get out the poison, give it some air.
If you are judged, toss it aside.
Peel off your mask, no need for false pride.
We are all human, feel your feelings, let's dare.
Cast aside the shame, buried tattered tears.

Pain summons strongly, it remembers my name.
I wish I could get out such a wicked game.
My words aren't sugary or saccharin sweet.
Floating azure waves from my head to my feet.
My hands to my ears such a deafening sound.
I must find my way to safer ground.

\.*~ ♡ ~*./

Abuse is plain evil, crumbling hearts.
Emotional or physical, cruel from the start.
A rag doll shredded thrown into the winds.
Never her fault, never her sin.
These words bleeding painful, sinking within.
Open dark curtains, let the light in.

Female warriors' spirits born of heat.
Endured so much pain, our wisdom is great.
We rise amongst the ashes, flames at our feet.
And yet we still love, there is no hate.
Our strength is unstoppable, that is not a debate.

I sit in the dark, black as the sky.
I sit and tremble wondering why.
I sit and ask, "How hard must I try?"
I sit and think will this all spin around.
I sit and say, "Faith will always be found."

Your kindness flows bejeweled trickling streams.
The rarest of diamonds, baby blues, silken greens.
Prisms of love reflect off my soul.
I feel your love, so tender, yet bold.
I cry, I stumble, hold me tight in our dreams.
Can you be my forever, so beautifully old?

\.*~ ♡ ~*./

Rainbows are the language of God.
After the rain, a miraculous start.
From azure blue skies to human hearts.
A myriad of colors, accept don't depart.

Drifting away like a summer breeze.
Tugging and twisting ropes wearing out.
Wanting my body to feel more at ease.
My heart sometimes in the land of doubt.
Where is the comfort I need to seize?
So many years, such thunderous shouts.
I close my eyes, I fly as I please.

Air is filled with panicky sounds.
My heart is sinking, nervous system pounds.
To be with another, can't escape or rebound.
Take a deep breath let the ocean flow through.
So many years, don't know what to do.
Just keep dreaming, my God will come through.

Beauty in the lens of the eye.
We see things differently, not a surprise.
From a beautiful sunset to the midnight sky.
One face an Adonis, another decries.
You may not think me beautiful, for that I won't cry.
What you feel most important,
Wherever exquisiteness lies.

\.*~♡~*./

I sit on a mountaintop alone much to bear.
My body in pain, I tear at my hair.
Only a veneer for what lurks below.
So many caverns, dark loud echoes.
Plunged no permission, not this frontier.
Sit and I struggle hard to swallow.
I look at tomorrow, new day, new prayers.

\.*~ ♡ ~*./

Can I kiss you at night under a starlit moon?
Your love for me such longings past noon.
Wash away my sorrows, a river's stream.
Come enter my soul, most vulnerable dreams.
Caress my scars, feel their heartache.
Take my hand, will never forsake.

I close my eyes sometimes full of fear.
Anxiety and pain many unwanted years.
My rituals a Godsend wipe away my tears.
The Divine in me whispers my name.
She tells me to dream, so much to gain.
She knows I will heal, is this real or a game?

We live in a world where we must accept.
God speaking through us, please don't forget.
Transgender souls as strong as they get.
Such warriors of courage, may they be blessed.
Hearts speaking through them, loud and clear.
True to themselves, despite any fears.

Some people just ignorant, no light of day.
Love and kindness must not go astray.
Let's extend to others still locked away.
Let's band together, banish the shame.
Go deep within, sing songs of praise.
We are all connected, divine energy the same.

Stumbling down, a thousand deaths.
Sometime feels like my very last breath.
Physical and metaphoric merge into one.
Original script perished, scalding hot suns.
My life got twisted need the right cap.
A genie in a bottle, is that the big lapse?

Love can battle the hardest fought wars.
Let down your swords, let kindness soar.
Sing out songs of peace let them roar.
We have it in us, no more detours.

I am human, sometimes torn.
I am human, sometimes I mourn.
I am human and sometimes feel joy.
I am human and sometimes feel worn.
I am human, I bleed not a toy.
I am human, prisms dim in the night.
I am human, morph from dark into light.

If I could undo these last many years,
Would I do it or leave it alone desert air?
Earthly body a resounding YES.
My soul may be on a different quest.
I am where I am, just accept it at best.
Sometimes easier said than done.
Kiss me gently sweet rising sun.

\.*~ ♡ ~*./

My friend is dear Mina.
My sweet kindred soul.
We've known each other before,
Different lifetimes ago.
We battled so long, red crimson swords.
Two poets in Paris, such gifts were bestowed.
We meet once again, a heavenly reward.

Feeling blue, life's vicissitudes.
A teeter-totter of emotions,
Dig through the commotion.
Distorted angles, adjustment in attitude.
Nothing is static,
Upside down, erratic.
Bear what you must, fade into the dust.
Showers of faith, I heal, I just must.

Your depth of love a breath of fresh air.
I lay my soul bare; you still want me here.
So judged all my life, so riddled and torn.
Even now, I am struggling, so very worn.
You want to know all; violins kiss my ears.
Your softness, sweet clouds dry up my tears.

\.*~ ♡ ~*./

Depression can hit some hard as a rock.
Be kind, it's difficult so many tough knocks.
Take off your shoes, walk in theirs.
You may feel blind sighted, so many tears.
Darkest of ink stains weary skin.
Compassion is God, let your heart in.

I need an escape net.
Let it fall from the sky.
Let it be big, ten miles wide.
Been trapped so long, so many regrets.
Pain playing music I want to forget.
I have to believe just take a deep breath.

If only you could take my pain away.
I know you would do it, such magical ways.
You said you would take it and make it your own.
I wept when I heard that, your love can melt stones.
I love you; I cherish you, my soul mate my friend.
Please hold my hand, let this never end.
Reach out and hold me; earth touches the sun.
Come and kiss me make me undone.

Hearing another's sounds of distress,
The anxiety, the panic, a life of its own.
Compassion in my heart,
But leaves me a mess.
Nervous system on steroids, I need a rest.
Sometimes shut down feeling like stone.
I need some sweet peace,
A life of my own.

Sometimes it seems life stands still.
Frozen icicles stuck on a hill.
Movement is beautiful, a delicate ballet.
Feeling inertia don't want to decay.
Seeds morph into flowers,
Imperceptible to the light of day.
Forever changing, our will, our way.

Your love as pure as the ocean is blue.
Sometimes I feel like a burden to you.
My words to you often filled with despair.
My pain, my suffering, you always still care.
You tell me it touches your heart when I share.
You melt me, I dissolve right into the air.
You tell me you love me, eyes misty tears.
Hold me, and kiss me, your heart is so rare.

I close my eyes, transported another place.
I see Monet, a splash of beauty and grace.
I walk in Paris clinking cobbled stone streets.
A smile from strangers, what a heavenly greet.
Another century, or a dream, celestial gates.

Sometimes damned if you do, damned if you don't.
Waters appear choppy, turn around just float.
Speak your voice loud, never say won't.
You are your strength, your wisdom, your hope.
Will not be stifled by some who just glare.
Disrespect is unwelcome, fly away midnight air.

\.*~ ♡ ~*./

The snow falls lightly, its crystals so pure.
I see your soul in them, colored prisms I adore.
Such beautiful auras a painting aglow.
Take my hand, soft rivers that flow.
Live moment by moment, our love only grows.

So, what is this thing we call "life?"
Sometimes full of joy, other times great strife.
Door's slam shut a bellowing sound.
Tears in our pockets, will we find safer grounds?
Beyond the "veil," a world yet unknown.
Seeds are planted, fresh harvests are grown.
What you put into it is what you reap.
Can be judged as bad or something so sweet.

I reach my hands out long winding roads.
I feel your embrace but hold to behold.
My heart always with you, yours with mine.
Beat down the door, obstacles, crushed vines.
Give me your vow, forever more,
We will find a way open heaven's door.

Take me away to some beautiful shore.
Let's close our eyes, musical ocean's roar.
Suspended in time, you are so far away.
Will I ever touch you, one fine summer's day?
I long for things, it's hard to endure.
In my cocoon, can I fly away?

\.*~ ♡ ~*./

Please whisper sweet nothings in my ear.
Speak to me of love, wipe away my tears.
Strip me naked, penetrate my mind.
Kiss my frailties, forever yours to find.
Raw and open crawl into my pain.
You touch me in ways, so hard to explain.

If I could orbit into space,
I would float like a star feeling no weight.
I would know a freedom, not felt before.
Come into my arms, let's open those doors.
I am my own savior, but you fill me with grace.
I can't wait to touch you and feel your embrace.

Feeling alone, pain is my plight.
Crawl into my body, darkest of nights.
I reach out to those battling this fight.
No want for sympathy, hearts' beacon of light.
Falling backwards, dizzying heights.
I pray for relief, my freedom, my life.

Is life an illusion, our brains being fooled?
We come back to learn, what's the big prize?
If we could only see beyond the "veil."
Tears may dry up, deep oceans so wise.
Mirages appear thick, but only thin air.
What appears so real, often a disguise.

Don't miss out!

Visit the website below and you can sign up to receive emails whenever Teri Dourmashkin publishes a new book. There's no charge and no obligation.

https://books2read.com/r/B-A-QHNBB-IHOCD

Connecting independent readers to independent writers.

Did you love *Beneath the Surface*? Then you should read *Skyward Ballet*[1] by Teri Dourmashkin and Mina Carroll!

[2]

"Skyward Ballet: A Symphony of the Soul" is a captivating anthology that weaves together the poetic voices of Teri Dourmashkin Ed.D and Mina Carroll.This collection is a celebration of friendship, a journey through the myriad landscapes of the human condition.Through their verses, Teri and Mina explore the complexities of love, the depths of sorrow, the solace of nature, and the eternal quest for meaning.Their poetry dances between the ethereal and the tangible, crafting a tapestry of emotion that invites readers to find pieces of themselves within its lines.With vivid imagery and profound insights, each poem serves as a beacon of hope, a reflection of life's beauty amidst its trials.This anthology is not merely a collection of poems but a shared experience,

1. https://books2read.com/u/31Bzx6

2. https://books2read.com/u/31Bzx6

a merging of horizons where two souls speak as one.It is an invitation to wander through the meadows of memory, to gaze upon the oceans of desire, and to soar towards the infinite sky of dreams."Skyward Ballet" promises to be a cherished companion for anyone who finds solace in words, a reminder that even in our deepest solitude, we are never truly alone.

About the Author

Dr. Teri Dourmashkin, Ed.D., is the founder of a minimalist skincare line, known for its natural ingredients and handcrafted batches. Alongside her skincare expertise, she is a passionate poet, blending beauty and wellness in both her professional and creative pursuits.terilove.com

Read more at terilove.com.